MAMA KNOWS BEST

Helping Mentors & Leaders Nurture Relationships with the Next Generation through Mama's Wisdom

JAQUAY REED

Mama Knows Best: Helping Mentors & Leaders Nurture Relationships with the Next Generation through Mama's Wisdom

For information contact:

Author: Jaquay Reed, jaquay@jalaree.com (www.jalaree.com)

Writing Coach & Self-Publishing Consultant: Sinyon Ducksworth, www.letthepaperspeak.com

Cover Designer: Brandon Jolly, www.brangraphicd.com

ISBN: 979-8-9905318-0-2

First Edition: May 2024

Contents

Introduction

As we journey through life, we gather wisdom from a multitude of sources—people, experiences, mistakes, and perhaps most profoundly, from the steady voice of a guiding figure. For many of us, that guiding figure is our mama. I personally carry with me the echoes of my mother's timeless wisdom, encapsulated in what I affectionately refer to as "Mama's quotes."

Growing up, I vividly recall the repetition of these quotes, sometimes to the point of annoyance. Yet, as I matured, I realized the profound impact they had on shaping my worldview and guiding my decisions. Mama's words weren't just platitudes; they were beacons of wisdom, lighting the path forward when uncertainty clouded my mind.

Reflecting on my teenage years, I initially dismissed Mama's quotes as redundant. Little did I know, they were quietly etching themselves into the fabric of my being, ready to emerge as guiding principles in moments of need. Even now, as an adult, I find myself instinctively reaching for these nuggets of wisdom in times of uncertainty or when faced with life's challenges.

There were moments when doubt crept in, and before I could

utter a word, Mama's voice would echo in my mind, urging me to press on and try. And in times of hurt or disappointment, her quotes served as a soothing balm, offering solace and perspective.

In this book, I invite you to embark on a journey of discovery—a journey fueled by the timeless wisdom encapsulated in Mama's quotes. Through personal anecdotes and reflections, I share how these simple yet profound phrases have shaped my life from adolescence to adulthood.

But this book isn't just about my journey—it's a tribute to the universal value of Mama's quotes. Every child is unique, yet the wisdom these quotes impart transcends differences in appearance, personality, and circumstance. Whether you're a parent, guardian, teacher, mentor, or simply someone who cares deeply about the next generation, this book offers a treasury of wisdom to share with the young people in your life.

Each quote is a catalyst for conversation, a spark that ignites meaningful dialogue between generations. In a social media driven world where communication is increasingly brief, mama's impactful quotes can offer a bridge between the wisdom of the past and the aspirations of the future.

As we navigate the complexities of a rapidly changing world, let us draw upon the timeless wisdom of Mama's quotes to guide, inspire, and empower the youth of today. Together, let us embark on a journey of shared learning, growth, and connection—a journey guided by the belief that Mama truly knows best.

Mama's Knows #1

"It's not so bad that it couldn't be worse"

Here is something my mama would say when I thought I experienced something bad or had a bad day. 'It's not so bad that it couldn't be worse'. Now this was not her being insensitive, but reflective in helping me think about my situation or my day. How compared to someone else that might be going through a tougher situation than mine, it might not be as bad as I thought it was. I adopted this quote over the years where it automatically pops into my mind and ushers out whatever I'm dealing with in that moment that I could count as bad because the circumstances could be worse. With this I learned that indeed there will be some rough days but embrace them and accept them just don't stay in that place. I actually think about how it could be worse and it has helped me to overcome those situations that seem unpleasant at first or at least have a more positive perspective regarding it where I am grateful for it.

Research Connection:

According to Mental Health Research Finding: "Gratitude" can be a source of many benefits that can help us in our situations. Gratitude is more than a natural response—it is an attitude that can help train our brain to be more attuned to positivity. Some benefits mentioned are:

Gratitude makes you more optimistic.

Gratitude makes you more forgiving.

Gratitude helps the battle against depression.

Gratitude helps improve sleep.

Gratitude helps lower high blood pressure.

Gratitude helps prevent overeating."

Source: *35 scientific benefits of gratitude: Mental Health Research Findings. Research.com. (2023, October 31).*

Key Takeaways:

Based on the research mentioned, "Gratitude"

- Helps us to be more optimistic about that situation that seems to be bad, but if we practice expressing gratitude, it's possible for us to go through that situation with a more positive outlook.
- Helps us to be more forgiving toward someone who may

have contributed to the situation that we find ourselves in. It could even be by our own doing that we find ourselves in a situation, but choosing to forgive allows us to move past it and not stay in that place harboring ill feelings.

- Helps us battle against depression, a place that readily awaits us to keep us bound from moving forward and overcoming the situation. Depression will undoubtedly make our situation worse than what is if we let it set in.

- How many of us lose sleep, worry and stress out which causes our blood pressure to spike, and/or start overeating when we focus on how bad our situation is? What if we were to do the opposite of those things and think about the positive things in our situation to be grateful for? We could potentially avoid troublesome health issues.

The research also found that gratitude has been scientifically recognized as a source of human strength (Emmons & Crumpler, 2000), this further encourages me to practice being grateful for every situation I encounter because it is a strength that you and I acquire. Gratitude can help us be strong mentally in our way of thinking to defeat all else that tries to keep us from seeing the best while in our situation.

Life Application:

*"When working with youth, when mentoring young people, or when supporting the young person in your life...**it's important to empower them to practice gratitude.**"*

- Give the young person a journal and encourage them to write out those things that are positive aspects in their life to focus on more so than the negative.
- Suggest that as they journal these things they also reflect on them from time to time as reminders to help keep them grounded.

Mama's Knows #2

"Nothing beats a failure, but a try"

I founded ***Created For Greatness*** *an outreach program for young girls between the ages of 9-16 and during one of our meetings in 2023, we talked about our fears. I asked, "What are some things you are afraid of?" One girl said she feared failing based on her observation of family members who had not succeeded at ventures they set out to accomplish. That looked like failure to her. I then asked the girls if they knew that it was important to fail at some things. This allowed me to share what Mama taught me growing up—nothing beats a failure but a try. I asked them if they knew what that meant. They looked around at each other, unsure.*

I explained it meant if you make the effort or attempt at that challenge you face, you won't fail because you gave it a try. Trying beats failing at something every time. Furthermore, you only fail at that thing if you give up or if you fail to try. I had them think about and imagine when they were babies how they began to grow to the point of a toddler who wanted to walk. I asked, "Did you just start walking because you could?" They all spoke up with a resounding, "No!" Then I asked, "Why?" They explained, "Because we couldn't walk, but we tried and probably fell a lot!" I said, "Exactly!" Toddlers don't just know how to walk but they try and fall plenty of times until they figure it out.

Trying *is putting one foot in front of the other like Mary Poppins or the train in the book The Little Engine That Could. If you never attempt to do something, you will never know the outcome of trying.*

Research Connection:

In 2018, research found that 60 percent of young people have trouble coping with the pressure to succeed.

However, various studies have shown that failure is by no means synonymous with a lack of accomplishment. Indeed, researchers from Northwestern University have decreed failure to be "the essential prerequisite for success," and a University of Arizona study says we **must** fail to learn, and failing 15 percent of the time is the "sweet spot."

"Striving to be perfect is likely complex," explains Daniel Madigan, a professor of psychology at York St. John University. "There is little wrong with wanting to do well and have high standards. The problems arise when achieving those standards is tied to one's sense of self."

Source: *Phelan, J. (2023, January 23). How failing could actually help us succeed. Discover Magazine. https://www.discovermagazine.com/mind/how-failing-could-actually-help-us-succeed*

Key Takeaways:

What really hit me is the percentage of young people who struggle with pressures to succeed, just like the girl in my outreach program who was afraid of failing. It's eye-opening to really sit with this truth that our little ones in our youth programs, churches, schools, and in our homes have these legitimate fears. The way they express these fears may look like "acting out", "lack of motivation", "disinterest" or "anxiety" and a combination of outward expressions. It also shows that we must demonstrate that **simply trying** is essential to success in whatever we do and failure is temporary as we keep trying to reach success. We can take the pressure off by refocusing young ones on "a simplified try" rather than a "grandiose ideal" of success. Trying will always exceed failing and is the most important step to any success.

Life Application:

"When working with youth, when mentoring young people, or when supporting the young person in your life, ***how can you encourage them to never give up during struggle seasons****?"*

- Show genuine interest by asking questions about their interests and ideas.

- Listen and hear them out. Try not to start formulating your response in your head while they are speaking. Sometimes the only response is to acknowledge you heard them, not an immediate solution.

- Offer words of affirmation to boost their morale and self-esteem.

- Don't hesitate to offer the proper support and resources when you see the young person struggling with an issue that is or may cause them physical harm. Become familiar with reputable crisis hotlines or centers (local or national). Build a community of support professionals that you can lean to when you feel overwhelmed or an issue the young person is struggling with is beyond your scope.

- Inform the young person that perfection is not the goal since we do not live in a perfect world, but always giving your best effort to anything worth achieving should be the mindset.

Mama's Knows #3

"Cook with love"

Growing up, I remember watching my mama prepare food for our family: breakfast, lunch, and dinner. I loved to watch her, so attentive, and taking pleasure in cooking for us. I especially loved it when she would serve the food, AND getting to eat it (I'm a certified foodie, check my IG)!

Mama serving the food was a delightful experience. She presented our meals so beautifully like a work of art and my dad's plate was the most stunning. His plate would look like a chef prepared it at a restaurant. Not only did her food look appetizing, but it tasted delicious. This has always piqued my curiosity because my mother has a very particular palette. She doesn't eat much of the foods she would prepare for us such as spaghetti with meat sauce, scrambled eggs, and tuna salad, yet she makes them all taste golden.

I can't remember my age when I asked her how she made everything she cooked taste so scrumptious without tasting the food. Like, where does one's motivation come from to create something so wonderful that they will never take part in themselves? She said, "You have to cook with love."

What does that mean? She loved and enjoyed cooking because it was centered on ***who*** *she was cooking for. It was an act of expressing her selfless love to us. Taking the time to prep the food, cook, plate it, and serve the food was creating this harmonious connection in her heart to us. It was her way of keeping the fire kindled in our hearts.*

Research Connection:

Studies suggest that the food prepared with love and effort is perceived to taste better. This is because our emotional perception of the taste of food is influenced by the amount of time and effort spent in the preparation of meals.

Dr. Christy Ferguson, a Birds Eye psychologist who led the study concluded that our awareness of the time and effort spent into preparing for the food we eat influences how we taste and enjoy the food.

Source: *Taylors, A. (2016, December 7). Science-backed reasons why food cooked with love is more delicious. University Herald. https://www.universityherald.com/articles/53686/20161207/science-backed-reasons-why-food-cooked-love-more-delicious.htm*

Key Takeaways:

This concept of *cooking with love* gives me a deeper understanding as to why whenever I witnessed Mama preparing food, I enjoyed it as much as I did. Loving effort truly makes a difference. The important lesson here is that when we do things with loving intention, it shows and it is felt. When we serve, create, and share with passion or compassion, we can find joy and fulfillment while filling the love tanks of others.

Life Application:

"When working with youth, when mentoring young people, or when supporting the young person in your life... ***it would be valuable to impart in them how love conquers all, not just cooking.****"*

- Make it fun by hosting a cooking lesson to demonstrate cooking with love using the previously mentioned tools of taking time and effort versus cooking without love—throwing the food together, and not putting in as much effort to see the results.

- Use the lesson as a framework for teaching time management (when we create proper time in our lives to carry out tasks, we don't have to be in rush-rush mode, which entices us to throw things together, turn in less half-done homework assignments, not giving even our passions full potential and space to grow and thrive.) Practicing time management is an act of love and self-love.

- You can also use the food lesson to show the kids how to transfer the key fundamentals to activities that interest them. Engage in this moment with them by making *loving* time and space for them to teach you about things they are passionate about (gaming, sports, jewelry making, art, etc.) and help them cultivate patience (emotional regulation) when they grow frustrated in their tasks.

Mama's Knows #4

"ALWAYS BE AWARE OF YOUR SURROUNDINGS, YOU NEVER KNOW WHO IS WATCHING"

GROWING UP IN THE inner city of Chicago's southside, I do not remember crime being as extreme as it has been over the past couple of decades. Mama being a mother, instinctively taught my sister and me to be aware of our surroundings at all times.

Mama remembers first mentioning this quote when she was teaching me a new level of responsibility. She gave me a copy of the house key since I would start walking home from school with my sister. Mama handed me the keys with a lesson, "Be aware of your surroundings, Jaquay. You never know who is watching you." She repeated it a few more times. Perplexed, I asked her why she kept repeating the same thing.

"People watch others for different reasons and in this case, you and your sister are young girls walking without an adult. I want you to be extra cautious to make sure you are aware that someone could be watching you and see you have a routine, so mix up your walking route. This will help you not be predictable." I needed to be aware of

my surroundings in this instance to guard myself against those who didn't mean me any good. Walking home from school I took this to heart. I would always look behind me, across the street, or even ahead of me. I still watch my surroundings to this day.

Research Connection:

"According to Miami Springs, FL Police department, situational awareness, in the most basic definition, is being aware of your surroundings and the activities going on around you. With more and more distractions in our everyday lives, it is important to have situational awareness. Whether you are driving down the road, at work, on vacation, or even at the mall you need to be aware of what is happening around you. This will allow you to take the necessary actions to avoid potential dangers. Not every situation can be prevented. In those cases, situational awareness may not help you avoid a dangerous situation, but it can increase your reaction time and thus improve the quality of the decisions you make. "

Source: *Situational awareness and personal safety. Situational Awareness and Personal Safety | City of Miami Springs Florida Official Website. (n.d.). https://www.miamisprings-fl.gov/police /situational-awareness-and-personal-safety*

Key Takeaways:

Situational awareness is not only an important safety measure but also a great way to give language to ideas and concepts you are teaching young ones about looking out for themselves. Educating young people isn't something we should leave up to an isolated event that only takes place in classrooms. Children learn by effectively applying knowledge to their real-world lives.

Life Application:

"When working with youth, when mentoring young people, or when supporting the young person in your life... ***beneficial to their safety, make them aware of situational awareness.*** *"*

- Ask the young person if they take time to notice their surroundings and based on their response ask them why or why not.

- Introduce the term *situational awareness* to them and allow them to explain what they think it means. Then allow the conversation to evolve from there, making sure to give the young person plenty of room to express themselves, ask questions, make observations, and explore actionable safety measures.

- Make sure they have a solid understanding and know the importance of their safety by being aware of their physical & virtual surroundings (at parties, at school events, walking in the community, playing outside, on public transportation, on social media, gaming platforms, etc.).

Mama's Knows #5

"DON'T SERVE ANYONE FOOD THAT YOU WOULDN'T EAT"

HAVE YOU EVER ORDERED food, let's say chicken from your favorite fast food restaurant and there was a chicken piece that looked weird, and unappetizing? This happened to me and all I could think was, "Why would they give me this piece of chicken; I know they had to see it." Whenever this happens to me, I'm reminded of Mama's advice, never to offer food to someone that I wouldn't eat myself. I remember Mama cutting and washing a chicken for a meal she was planning to prepare. She tossed a piece to the side and said she was going to throw it away. I asked her why she would do that. She pointed out that the flesh of the chicken looked bruised and she wouldn't eat it nor would she serve it to someone else. This has helped me in different areas of life, not just with food. If I come across something that I find discouraging, harmful, or destructive, and I know others might be similarly affected, I would voice my concerns immediately or refrain from sharing anything I consider damaging.

Research Connection:

Let's take it to the Bible:

- "Do to others as you would like them to do you." **(Luke 6:31, NLT)**
- "Treat others the same way you want them to treat you." **(Luke 6:31, AMP)**
- "Let no one seek [only] his own good, but [also] that of the other person." **(1 Corinthians 10:24, AMP)**
- "So do the good things for other people that you would want them to do for you. That is true for everything you do. That is what God's Law and the message of God's prophets teach us." **(Matthew 6:12, EASY)**

Key Takeaways:

It is without question that we as human beings will look out for ourselves, but we should also look out for others and their best interests. This may not apply to every situation, but it applies to every person. We create a better world for ourselves and our children by simply treating others as we want to be treated. Imagine a community, a city, a country where everyone practiced this one simple concept. What an amazing world would we live in...

Life Application:

*"When working with youth, when mentoring young people, or when supporting the young person in your life...**empower them to practice authentic giving.**"*

- Teach young people that it isn't sufficient to just give something away because they don't want it for themselves. They should practice giving the very best and how to find joy in that type of giving.

- Help young people find fulfillment and joy in giving by having them participate/volunteer in outreach programs. Even if young individuals receive services from an outreach program or a youth shelter, it doesn't mean they cannot learn the importance of helping others. In fact, volunteering could give them a sense of dignity and appreciate the value of giving and receiving as an interwoven act of love and kindness.

Mama's Knows #6

"You can't say no one told you"

As a child, I was taught right from wrong, knowing the difference between good and bad. At times of instruction, Mama would say "You can't say no one told you." As an adult, this has helped me over the years to retain as well as heed any instruction that is communicated to me so I can be accountable for my actions and responses in different situations.

For example, I was taught not to lie. If I chose to tell a lie and the truth was found, I'd have to face the consequences. There are consequences for everything that we do in life whether positive or negative. I have experienced both from the choices I have made in my life. This lesson taught me to own up to the things I did that put me in unpleasant situations, "Cause you couldn't say no one told you." Sometimes we take on a victim's role so we can avoid facing our mess-ups, which only prolongs the struggle season of growth.

Reflecting on past experiences, there have been several instances where adhering to a pivotal piece of advice has led to great results. Whether it's the simple act of double-checking work for errors or the more complex task of maintaining composure under pressure, these key lessons have often paved the way to success. Can you think of a few of these moments in your life?

And what about a negative result when you chose to do something you knew was not the best idea? Although painful to face, think about how much better you were able to recover when you owned up and moved forward.

Research Connection:

Excerpt from the article, "How and Why to Help Your Kid Create a Culture of Personal Accountability" details:

Anne Franck once said, "Parents can only give good advice or put them on the right paths, but the final forming of a person's character lies in their own hands." She was speaking about personal accountability. Every kid needs to know that actions have consequences and that he is responsible for his behavior. Failing to hold our kids accountable for their actions and their behavior can have a far-reaching impact on their ability to be personally accountable in the childhood years and beyond.

Source: *Sanya Pelini, Ph. D. (2018, October 9). How and why to help your kid create a culture of personal accountability - raising-independent-kids. Raising. https://raising-independent-kids.com/how-and-why-to-help-your-kid-create-a-culture-of-personal-accountability/*

Key Takeaways:

The article excerpt helps to put accountability in perspective. Parents' role in giving good advice or directing a child on the right path is what my mama was doing in speaking, "You can't say no one told you." But this lesson isn't limited to parents, any person who is offering sound wisdom to a young person is beneficial. Although our world has changed drastically due to technology, there's one principle that still should remain true in our lives—it takes villages to raise children. We are all accountable for supporting a young person's healthy development. This could mean the way we show up online, the posts we make, and how we handle ourselves before them. When leaders in positions of authority avoid acknowledging their public mistakes, despite knowing they're in the wrong, they inadvertently teach passively through their actions.

Kids see us. They need to know actions have consequences and the significance of being held accountable reaches far past childhood, something I can attest to. Being held accountable helped my mama, then she taught it to me, and we continue to pass the buck.

Life Application:

*"When working with youth, when mentoring young people, or when supporting the young person in your life...**empower them to understand what it means to be accountable for their actions.**"*

- Explain how there are good (positive) consequences and not-so-good (negative) consequences for every choice we make.

- Use yourself as an example: Share your personal, *couldn't say no one told me*, story.

- Ask them if they want to share one of their own.

Mama's Knows #7

"Keep living"

I remember one afternoon a few years ago my sister and I were in her car headed home when I received a call from our 20-year-old nephew. I answered and put him on speakerphone so my sister could be part of the conversation. Every chance we get, we encourage our nephew to keep doing great things. We went into encouragement mode during this particular call and I distinctly remember my sister saying to him, "As my mother would say, Keep Living." I remember her saying she didn't understand what it meant the times Mom would say it until she started to experience life for herself. Have you ever had a moment or two in your teenage or young adult life when you thought you had it all figured out but you didn't? You didn't figure it out until after you lived through some things–KEEP LIVING. This helped my sister become wiser and more capable of handling different life situations. I believe as we live, we will continue to learn how to ***do life*** *better. Making each day better than before without trying to have it all figured out. Each day is different, each situation is different, generations change and so does society amongst so many other things. We as people are continually evolving so we need to keep living to learn what's next.*

It's like quote #21...you live and you learn.

Research Connection:

"Always remember what you have learned. Your education is your life – guard it well." **(Proverbs 4:13, GNT)**

"People use different words to describe the meaning of a lived experience. Examples include stories, past experiences, and background. A brief from the U.S. Department of Health and Human Services defines lived experiences as the "representation and understanding of an individual's human experiences, choices, and options."

Source: *The power of lived experiences: Youth engaged 4 change. The Power of Lived Experiences | Youth Engaged 4 Change. (n.d.). https://engage.youth.gov/blog/power-lived-experiences*

Key Takeaways:

As we live each day, we encounter new experiences. I think about babies—how they grow from being held to crawling and moving about independently. Babies think it's the best thing ever until they take their first steps and their little world explodes with new possibilities. Then it's hard to keep them still after that. Could it be that a baby's "lived experience" of movement and observation while being carried around helped them understand that free movement was possible and that curiosity led to crawling, then walking, and likely running? We have to "keep living" to experience life with all its ups and downs. No matter how long we live, we will never have it all figured out, but we can build upon what we learn to help us get to the next stage of our life journey.

Life Application:

*"When working with youth, when mentoring young people, or when supporting the young person in your life...**cheer them on to embrace lived experiences.**"*

- You might ask the young person what activities they are good at or which activities they have mastered (games, sports, hobbies).
- After listing their proficiencies, ask them why they believe they are so good at it.
- Ask if they believe there could be more to learn/experience and how they think it will help them in the future.

Mama's Knows #8

"God don't like ugly"

"God don't like ugly," is what Mama would say to deter me from doing something that was not in my best interest...ugly. I listened to Mama, but there was one time she wasn't around and I did something ugly. When I was 7 years old, my Granny would watch me after school. One afternoon we went to the grocery store and I was told beforehand that I could not have any candy. I heard it and said, "Okay," but right before the checkout counter there was a display of all sorts of delectable candies. The one sweet treat that caught my eye was the Ring Pop. I'd seen the jumbo diamond-shaped candy rings in commercials but had never had it before. Well as Granny was checking out and conversing with the cashier, I was behind her standing in front of the candy section contemplating if I should grab a ring pop. Nervousness clinched my stomach as time was running out since she was almost done. The desire was overwhelming, so I grabbed one and didn't tell Granny.

Stealing. I learned a valuable lesson that day...it does not pay to steal 'anything' because God don't like ugly. Once we got back to Granny's house, I was so anxious to get out of the car, trying not to panic. I ran upstairs to the bathroom and locked the door. I knew I had done something wrong and thought I had gotten away with it. I hadn't noticed which flavor I grabbed, but as I took it out of my pocket, it was my favorite flavor...cherry. My mouth was watering as I began to unwrap it thinking how great this was going to taste. I was smiling as I put the ring on my finger. Gazing at the big red diamond-shaped treat, I went in to taste it and to my surprise it was disgusting. I was so disappointed. It did not taste good at all. It tasted like syrup mixed with artificial cherry flavoring that weirdly clashed. I looked at myself in the bathroom mirror and had tears in my eyes, thinking to myself, "This is why you were taught not to steal. God don't like ugly." I am grateful for this experience as a kid because it was a lesson learned that I will never forget. Something so simple helped me realize stealing doesn't benefit me but could hurt me and prove unrewarding in the end.

Research Connection:

What does the word "ugly" mean? Merriam-Webster's dictionary has 4 definitions. For this quote, the most appropriate definition is #2 - morally offensive or objectionable.

"For the Lord is [absolutely] righteous, He loves righteousness (virtue, morality, justice); The upright shall see His face." **(Psalms 11:7, AMP)**

Key Takeaways:

Referencing Psalms 11:7 is one way of exploring how God don't like ugly (#2 definition from Websters Dictionary - morally offensive or objectionable) but loves righteousness (morality). This is simply said and is what Mama wanted me to understand as a child. It wasn't until the ugly act of stealing in my adolescence that I understood the quote, *God don't like ugly*.

Life Application:

*"When working with youth, when mentoring young people, or when supporting the young person in your life...**it would be advantageous to get their perspective on righteousness.**"*

- Engage the young person in conversation by asking them what the quote "God don't like ugly" means to them (be prepared to get the funnies and let it be a relaxed conversation).

- Ask open-ended questions: Pick their brain / get to know them / explore their knowledge or mindset. Be more observant and allow them to lead the conversations, with you providing the structure.

- Follow up with what it means to you, and share your own "God don't like ugly," story where you got caught up in an *ugly* situation. Close the conversation with what that situation taught you and connect it with a larger takeaway for them.

Mama’s Knows #9

“DON'T YOU FEEL BETTER WHEN YOU SMILE”

I AM A PERSON who loves to smile. I think I can attribute that to plenty of things from my childhood, my relationship with God, and of course my mama. As far as I can remember, I smiled most of my childhood except for when things didn’t go my way. But Mama would teach my sister and me to smile when we were in moments of unhappiness.

I asked her about this recently and she remarked, "I had to tell your sister to smile more than I did you." There was usually a mild repercussion if we did not smile. So, we would smile reluctantly. She would then follow up with, “Now, don’t you feel better when you smile?”

I asked Mama why it was so important to instill this in us. She said, “I learned when you frown you are using more muscles in your face, but when you smile you use fewer muscles. Plus, whatever you feel like you want to be unhappy about is not so bad that it couldn’t be worse” (Quote #1). I remember hearing about using more muscles to frown than smile in school as a kid. I will say that I believe being encouraged to smile as a kid when things didn't go my way helped me overall to smile no matter my situation. That's not to say I initially will smile in a circumstance that does not automatically trigger a smile, but eventually, I will smile to help myself get through it. Because truth be told, I do feel better when I smile. How do you feel when you smile versus when you frown?

Research Connection:

"In a recent paper published in Nature Human Behavior, an international collaboration of researchers led by Stanford research scientist Nicholas Coles found strong evidence that posed smiles can, in fact, make us happier."

"Coles further explains that smiling by no means can overcome something like depression, but "the stretch of a smile can make people feel happy and the furrowed brow can make people feel angry; thus, the conscious experience of emotion must be at least partially based on bodily sensations."

Source: *University, S. (2022, October 14). Posing smiles can brighten our mood. Stanford News. https://news.stanford.edu/2022/10/20/posing-smiles-can-brighten-mood/*

"The mechanics of how smiling might make us feel happier aren't yet known," said Coles, but it could be, "if you activate a smile the peripheral nervous system tells the rest of the system that happiness is happening and it tries to catch up."

Source: *TodayShow. (2022, October 21). Simply smiling may make us feel happier, new study suggests. TODAY.com*

. *https://www.today.com/health/behavior/smiling-may-make-us-feel-happier-new-study-suggests-rcna53295*

Key Takeaways:

The research reveals that smiling actually can make us feel better just like Mama said. Smiling is usually an expressed emotion that symbolizes happiness or joy outwardly. It's also fascinating to learn that something as simple as a smile could trigger our "nervous" system internally, sending a message through the rest of our body. Makes sense why one would feel better when smiling. The feel good hormones (dopamine, serotonin, endorphins, and oxytocin) are getting released!

Life Application:

*"When working with youth, when mentoring young people, or when supporting the young person in your life...**knowing that a simple smile can alter their feelings can be quite beneficial for kids.**"*

- When you're helping a young person process through a trying time, ask them to try smiling as an experiment.
- Ask them how they feel after smiling.
- Consider sharing how this act influences your feelings during moments of sadness.

Mama's Knows #10

"Mama knows"

This quote is my sister's favorite, and I will say one of mine as well. My sister has taken this quote and used it in moments of sorrow. With tears flowing, this quote injects humor for her that turns sorrow into joy and tears into laughter. Every mother has a way of comforting her child and "Mama knows" is an endearing sentiment that our mom used with us. Though Mama has said this to me during various situations in my childhood, one incident that took place during my adulthood stands out in my memory the most and meant the world to me.

When I was around 27 years old, I bought my first home, a condo in Oak Lawn, IL. I'd never rented at a commercial property/complex prior to that so I was unaware of how owning a condo worked. My one bedroom, one bath unit was on the first floor and I was excited to officially have my own place. There was an issue with the a/c wall unit that was noted on the inspection to be repaired or replaced by the seller after closing. A few months after I moved in, the sellers sent a couple of guys to look at the a/c unit. One of the guys told me that they would need a key to get in and I told him he would just need to contact me for access.

I asked my parents what they thought, and Mama said I should not need to give them a key because I am the owner. Dad said he wasn't sure because he didn't know how condos worked since it was like an apartment complex. Hesitantly, I ended up giving the guy a key to one of the two locks on my door during the next visit. I told him to contact me to schedule a day when he would need access and that the one key would not get him full entry. My decision did not make sense, but at that time, I was confused and should have listened to Mama.

I came home from work one day and my place was broken into. As I opened the door, I saw that my living room was ransacked. I was in disbelief just standing at the door looking around and when I realized what had happened my heart was broken. I called my friend who had just dropped me off at home from carpooling asking him to come back to stay with me. I called the police and my parents. My parents arrived and the police shortly after. Once I was done giving my statement, it was all sinking in. I looked around seeing my place turned upside down, the police going through everything and I just burst into tears with a loud wail. Mama immediately grabbed me and embraced me saying with empathy, "Mama Knows," over and over as I cried in her chest. Those words at that moment of my emotional breakdown gave me an assured feeling of love and security I desperately needed.

Research Connection:

"Parenting expert Dr. Michele Borba, the author of 12 Simple Secrets Real Moms Know, agrees that "oneness" is at the root of mother's intuition. "The reason that we're able to act on our intuition is that it's not just that gut feeling," she says. "It's based on empathy. We're so tuned in to them that we're actually—it's called stepping into their shoes—feeling with them. You're in communion with the other person.""

"That's why mother's intuition is most acute in times of distress, says Dr. Judith Orloff, an assistant clinical professor of psychiatry at UCLA and the author of Second Sight, a book examining intuition."

Source: *Aydin, D., Hamlin, R., & Editors, T. (2015, March 20). A mother knows. Guideposts. https://guideposts.org/positive-living/friends-and-family/parenting/children/a-mother-knows/*

Key Takeaways:

I find it comforting that parenting expert Dr. Michele Borba relates oneness as the "root" of a mother's intuition, a mother's knowing. As I reflect, I know I can feel my mother's *knowing* in my bones. On many occasions, she has undoubtedly proven that acute mother's awareness in times of trouble is true in her coming to my rescue because "Mama knows."

Whether or not a young person is your child, you can still tap into your intuition with them to avoid missing an opportunity to be there for them and further connect with them. Tap into your "withitness." This classroom management strategy, *withitness*, is effective because students might believe their teacher has eyes in the back of their heads, given how the teacher seems to be aware of everything happening, even when not facing the class.

Or have you ever called your parent or someone you loved and you could tell something was wrong from the conversation or tone? That's your intuition kicking in. Although you may not be a mom or even a woman, you are human with human instincts and the powerful ability to tap into other humans, if you take the time to listen with your whole self. You can also cultivate this skill, and practice emotional intelligence strategies to grow in this area. Also, tapping into yourself and becoming more self aware will help.

Life Application:

*"When working with youth, when mentoring young people, or when supporting the young person in your life...**tap into your human intuition.**"*

- Use your intuition by paying attention to the young person in your life. Read the room, so to speak. Don't be the principal from the movie, Dangerous Minds, who was so focused on rule and order, that he missed a kid coming to him for help.

- Use your intuition by listening to what the young person is saying or trying to say to engage them in conversation. It is important to keep in mind that what they say and how they behave may not reflect what they actually feel inside.

- Even if your head is full of criticisms and instruction, use your intuition to give the young person words of encouragement and comfort when needed.

Mama Knows #11

"WHAT YOU PUT INTO LIFE IS WHAT YOU GET OUT"

As I think about this quote, I hear Mama's voice saying it. I know how it helped me in life, but I asked Mama what these wise words meant to her. She shared with me, "When you look and think about what you want out of life then contemplate how you would or should go about getting it...the effort you 'put forth to get it' is the ***putting in*** *part. The fruit or the result of your efforts is the 'what you get out' part." This makes me think of "You reap what you sow" or "cause and effect." Every day we are putting in some form of work, whether work at school, work on the job, work in our ministry, work on our athletics team, or work in our community. We put in that work to produce a positive outcome and benefits for ourselves, our family, and hopefully for society. What were you taught about life to 'put in' the world? What did you get out of it? Hopefully, we are taught to put positive work into life and to remember that even though things don't always seem to have a positive outcome every time, those are the little bumps in the road we must experience to get the good out of what we put in.*

Research Connection:

"You may be familiar with the Biblical quote "You reap what you sow." The things you do are like planted seeds, and those seeds produce a crop which is the result of your actions." **(Galatians 6:7-8, TPT)**

The quote is an example of the cause and effect relationship. Your action, sowing good or bad seeds, produces a reaction, a healthy or rotten harvest.

A cause is an **action**, and the effect is the resulting **reaction**.

- A cause is a catalyst, a motive...that brings about a reaction.

A cause **instigates** an effect.

- An effect is a condition, occurrence, or result generated by one or more causes.
- Effects are **outcomes**.

A cause is ***why*** something happens. An effect is ***what*** happened.

Source: *Cause and effect: Definition, meaning, and examples.* ProWritingAid. (n.d.). https://prowritingaid.com/cause-and-effect

Key Takeaways:

What you put into life is what you get out of life is another way of thinking of cause and effect or reaping and sowing. When I have to make certain decisions as simple as eating, I think about what food I want to eat and how it might make me feel afterwards (practicing mindfulness). What I consume will affect how my body feels, functions, responds in days or over the course of years. It's a matter of do I want positive or negative results from the choices I make.

Life Application:

*"When working with youth, when mentoring young people, or when supporting the young person in your life...**help them comprehend that their choices have consequences or there is a cause and effect to the choices they make.**"*

- Ask the young person to list 3 of their responsibilities.
- Then ask what is the result of them doing or not doing these tasks.
- Next, ask what they think the result would be if they did the opposite.
- Help tie their example to cause and effect as related to the quote. Teach them that goals are indeed achievable and they happen by sowing small daily seeds.

Mama Knows #12

"YOUR BEAUTY COMES FROM THE INSIDE...IF YOU ARE BEAUTIFUL ON THE INSIDE, SO WILL YOU BE ON THE OUTSIDE"

DURING DIFFERENT OCCASIONS IN my mama's childhood she would hear her mom or aunts say things about others, "Like she is a pretty girl, but she sure has some ugly ways, or he would be handsome if he would act nicer." So mama related that to a Bible verse in Matthew where Jesus calls out the pharisees about their toxic inner selves verses their beautiful outer appearance. Can you think of an encounter you may have had with someone where your good first impressions of them conflicted with how they actually behaved? Maybe they weren't kind in speaking or their actions revealed the opposite of who they presented themselves to be. I know when I come across people like that it's not me being judgmental of them, but my awareness to never judge a book by its cover.

Research Connection:

"It will be very bad for you, teachers of God's law and Pharisees. You are hypocrites! You are like a grave that has nice white paint on the outside and it looks beautiful. But on the inside it is full of bones and disgusting things." **(Matthew 23:27, EASY)**

"When they arrived, Samuel saw Jesse's son Eliab. Samuel thought, 'I am sure that the LORD has chosen this man to be king.' But the LORD said to Samuel, 'Do not look at how handsome or how tall Eliab is. I have not chosen him. The Lord does not look at people in the way that people do. People look at the face and body of a person. But the Lord sees what they are like inside." **(1 Samuel 16:6-7, EASY)**

Key Takeaways:

Like the biblical Samuel, people in general look at the outer appearance (skin deep/surface level), but God looks deeper. He is looking in our hearts (Luke 6:45, GNT). What is in our hearts? Good or bad will flow externally and will overshadow the physical presentation that displays beauty.

Life Application:

*"When working with youth, when mentoring young people, or when supporting the young person in your life...**instill in them good character**."*

- Ask the young person if they know what good character

means or what it means to have integrity. Explain if needed.

- Ask them if they believe they practice good character. If so, give examples.
- Explain the importance of good character and how it will take them far in life.

Mama Knows #13

"Follow your first mind"

Mama always said to follow your first mind. Your first mind? Your first thought is what she was referring to. For a few years, I operated a part-time mobile childcare business and on September 21, 2021, upon leaving a client's house, I got in my car to go home when the thought to call my grandma came to mind. I picked up the phone to call then I told myself, "You're tired, so just call her tomorrow." Immediately after that thought, I heard a still small voice say..."Call her today." Before I started my car to drive off, I called my grandma. We had a nice conversation, but I could tell from her dialog that she was a little different. Before ending the call, I told her that I loved her and I hoped that she would feel better and no longer feel tired. After our call, I said a prayer for her and kept on my way home.

The next day, I got a call from my sister. She had Mama on the other line. Mama told us that our grandma had passed away. Upon receiving the news, all I could think was, "Oh my goodness, if I had waited to call Grandma yesterday, I might not have had the privilege to talk to her before she passed." My 'first mind' to call her was the one that I followed. Some people might call following your first thought as a sixth sense, intuition, etc. I have learned to really pay attention to my first thoughts in some decisions. I like to believe that it is the way the Holy Spirit or divine spiritual intelligence helps me to make the best decisions when they really matter. This will lead us to quote #14: "Never put off tomorrow what you can do today."

Research Connection:

Studies show, "listening to your intuition is, as Albert Einstein put it, "a sacred gift," something to not just honor but pursue and seek out. Our intuition is a gateway to deeper creativity, richer self-expression, better decision-making, enhanced self-awareness, improved mental health, and even fortified physical wellbeing."

"Intuition is often talked about as existing on two planes - there's the day-to-day intuition" like making choices of whether to wear a blue or green shirt; a powerful "small window into who we are and what we want."

Then there is the deeper second plane: "Knowing something is happening, or that you should do something, without physical [hard] proof you're right."

Researchers believe, "Intuition isn't just "made-up" feelings, it's based on neurochemicals fired when our brain subconsciously senses patterns. It draws on our memory archives, comparing what we see, feel, and experience now with what we have seen, felt, and experienced in the past. It nudges us to take action toward what we want to see, hear and experience."

Source: Lockerman, C. (2022a, July 4). *Learning to listen to your* *intuition*. Rock Creek Counseling. https://www.rockcreekcounseling.com/blog/9xnrafatdd6bfcpstkm6smn2n7drdz

Key Takeaways:

Here we are back referencing intuition like in quote #10 (mothering intuition). This new perspective reveals that intuition is your psyche recalling previous occurrences and indicators which helps our brains make decisions, quickly gathering information from our subconscious to urge us towards an action that sometimes defies logical reasoning. So there seems to be times when we are in situations that our "intuition" will kick-in automatically. Do you remember a time when your intuition turned on? Did you pay attention to it or didn't think much about it? What was the result?

Life Application:

"When working with youth, when mentoring young people, or when supporting the young person in your life... ***help them recognize their intuition.****"*

- First, model intuitive living by including self-awareness practices in your own life.
- Attempt to spark the young person's intuition with a scenario that would help jog their thoughts to what instantly comes to mind.
- Ask the young person what thought comes to mind and how it differs from how they might normally respond. If verbal expression is difficult, give them opportunities to

express themselves using creativity arts and crafts, nature exploration, etc.

- Give patience, use affirming words, and remember this is not a time to judge or get the young person to give "right" answers (for your approval). Kids do not operate in intuitive thought when they are trying to conform, comply, or they do not feel they are in a safe space to express themselves freely. Help them to find their voice through gentle mentoring.

Mama Knows #14

"NEVER PUT OFF TOMORROW WHAT YOU CAN DO TODAY"

A FAMOUS QUOTE ATTRIBUTED to Benjamin Franklin, *"Never put off tomorrow what you can do today," is my all-time favorite quote. This quote has stuck with me based on a situation that my mother encountered as a young adult.*

Mama shared with me that this quote became wisdom for her after a very personal experience. She explained, "If it's on your heart and mind to do, don't put it off until later. Waiting until later may cause you heartache or regret."

At 22 years old, Mama was taught this precious lesson. After I was born, one of Mama's paternal aunts, Aunt Callie, asked her every week to bring me over to see her. Mama would happily say, "Yes," with intentions to do so, but did not make it a top priority.

I was 4 months old when she learned Aunt Callie had passed away without her getting to meet me. Mama said her heart was crushed when she found out. She couldn't believe it. She thought she had time.

Though she was distraught that she had missed the opportunity to introduce me to her aunt, she did not stay in a place of regret. Instead, this moment inspired her to never put off for the future what she could do in the present.

Research Connection:

"In the past 20 years, the peculiar behavior of procrastination has" become a popular topic for researchers. Interestingly, "psychological researchers now recognize that there's far more to it than simply putting something off until tomorrow. True procrastination is a complicated failure of self-regulation: experts define it as the voluntary delay of some important task that we intend to do, despite knowing that we'll suffer as a result."

Source: Jaffe, E. (2013, March 29). *Why wait? the science behind procrastination*. Association for Psychological Science - APS. https://www.psychologicalscience.org/observer/why-wait-the-science-behind-procrastination

Key Takeaways:

The article mentions that "true" procrastination is a voluntary delay of an important task. Of course, we can never know what may lie ahead in our journey, like missing an opportunity to visit a loved one, one more time before they pass away. Like my mom, we often gain deeper clarity in taking action on our intentions after we've suffered a hard consequence. The realization of unintentional procrastination leads to a moment of growth in better prioritizing and following through on our word.

Life Application:

*"When working with youth, when mentoring young people, or when supporting the young person in your life...**teach them the importance of follow through.**"*

- Offer them a planner or help them create a tool that will help them organize their to-do's, tasks, and goals.

- Show interest by asking them if they have any tasks or goals they have set to accomplish and inquire of them if they are on track. Follow up with open-ended questioning of what is hindering them if they are not on track.

- As a follow up ask how they plan to execute a big overarching goal they have in mind. Sometimes "dream" goals can feel too far away to touch or impossible to realize because it may take many steps to get there. This can lead to procrastination or giving up. Help them process through this.

- Offer to be their accountability partner.

Mama Knows #15

"IT TAKES ALL KINDS TO MAKE THE WORLD GO-ROUND"

WHAT IS YOUR PROFESSION? Are you creative? What are you passionate about? If you can answer any one of these questions, there are over 7 billion people in the world including yourself that contribute to that same passion one way or another. When I think about the different professions, creative works, discoveries, nuisances, technologies, and so on it makes me think about Mama saying, "It takes all kinds to make the world go round." When I see a first responder on television attending to someone who is injured, I know that is not for me. I wouldn't be able to function. As nurturing and helping as I could be, the stress in that scenario would override my ability to provide care. I enjoy watching the construction of buildings from start to finish because carpentry fascinates me but it is another profession that is outside of my skillset. My passion is caring for kids. I have had different people share with me that they don't know how I do it, but caring for children, playing with them, and loving them comes easy to me and is natural for me. Whatever the profession, skill, or ability–each one of us impacts the world's operation by our diversity.

Research Connection:

USenglish.com references this quote as an Idiom meaning, "Diversity is essential – the world would be incomplete if everyone were alike."

"Even if you're not trying to solve world hunger or global warming, brainstorming ways to help your community can make a big difference. When we help others, it doesn't stop with us. Studies have found that when we help others, those around us are more likely to help, too...In that way, one person's actions really can change the world for good."

Source: *Discover the meaning of "it takes all kinds to make a world."* UsingEnglish.com. (n.d.).

"In terms of physical benefits, making a difference in your community can increase your lifespan. Researchers found that seniors who regularly served others lived longer, on average, than those who didn't."

Source: *How to change the world: One person can make a lasting impact.* Waterford.org. (2023, June 7). https://www.waterford.org/education/how-to-change-the-world/

Key Takeaways:

People invented the airplane and figured out how to make it fly along with other advancements in technology. There was once no such thing as a physical computer but now computers are used in almost everything we touch. We may not be able to make major changes like those, but starting in our communities can have a positive impact in a big way. You could be mentoring the person who creates a life-changing invention that changes the world. Is there any way you have contributed to your community? Were there others who also wanted to help? Others have supported me with my non-profit outreach program *Created For Greatness* (https://created4g.com/).

After referencing the research and learning how making a difference in our community can increase our lifespan, this fact is an additional motivator, influencing us to play our part in making the world *go round.*

Life Application:

*"When working with youth, when mentoring young people, or when supporting the young person in your life...**encourage them to practice giving back to the community.**"*

- Ask the young person to write down three ways they would like to help a person, group, or community outreach.
- Of the three, help them choose the one that would be easiest to implement.
- Have them write down ways to get started while you offer ideas.
- Encourage your young mentees to do their research.

- Work with them on their *follow through.*
- Let them know that taking this first action is a stepping stone to open doors for the other ideas on their list.

Mama Knows #16

"As you learn better you do better"

I asked my sister what this Mama's quote meant to her. She said simply not repeating mistakes and taking the lessons learned from her mistakes to better navigate life. There have been times when I have repeated the same mistake over and over again. But when I decided to learn from it, I grew from it as well and didn't fall into the same traps. Is there a time you can think of when you learned from a mistake? How long did it take you to learn from it? I asked my sister these questions and she shared how Mama taught us as teenagers not to get credit cards, but she chose to do it anyway. Not just one, but a few. From this, she accumulated debt. It wasn't until years later during a financial education class that she realized the importance of not having credit cards to be debt-free. Learning from that experience she closed the credit cards she had and was able to pay off her credit card debt over time. "I no longer rely on credit cards, but on God to provide all my needs" my sister explained.

Research Connection:

"One thing researchers have found...is that the brain creates a specific kind of brain activity when a person makes a mistake. This activity, called the error-related negativity or ERN, happens almost at the same time that the error is made. It is as if the brain already knows we are making a mistake within fractions of a second, before we are even aware of it."

"Many scientific studies have found that, after making a mistake, we respond more slowly in the next round. This might be because the brain is trying to give itself more time, to avoid making the same mistake again. The stronger the ERN is after an error, the slower the response in the next round tends to be."

Source: Authors Marlene Meyer, Authors Katherine Diane Andrade, Authors Richard J. Addante, & Authors Bianca Westhoff. (n.d.). *Learning from mistakes: How does the brain handle errors?*. Frontiers for Young Minds. https://kids.frontiersin.org/articles/10.3389/frym.2020.00080

Key Takeaways:

The research shows us that even our brains are geared to adapt and learn from making mistakes. It may take one time or a few times to learn from the mistake, but the brain activity we unknowingly experience helps us to practice self-awareness and develop the necessary skills to move away from making decisions that lead to the same negative outcomes. Though making mistakes is part of human nature, it's great to know we are equipped to learn from them and will be that much better off from the experience.

Life Application:

"When working with youth, when mentoring young people, or when supporting the young person in your life... ***help them realize mistakes will happen, but learning from them is part of positive self-improvement.****"*

- Have a discussion with your young people about mistakes they learned from and things they still have a hard time learning from.

- Share something you have conquered and one thing you still struggle with to give them the courage to open up. The point is not perfection but growth. And sometimes we have to bump our heads a few times to grow.

Mama Knows #17

"Make-up is used to enhance your natural beauty"

I thought it would be fun to ask my sister her thoughts on this quote because she took an interest in make-up early on in her young adulthood. She said she was never really a make-up girl, but eyeshadow was an attractive style that caught her eye. She explained it adds color and brings out the hidden beauty of the eyes. Then she learned foundation is good for evening skin tone, but as she got more mature in age, she preferred her natural beauty with all its imperfections over using the foundation. She mentioned that the foundation changed her appearance more than she desired. As she sees the natural beauty of women on TV or social media contrasted with their made-up faces from cosmetics, she thinks about the drastic difference in appearance and how their natural beauty is very becoming. She now believes what Mama taught us, that makeup only enhances what is already there.

Mama has never been one to wear much make-up. She generally will apply lipstick and maybe foundation, but I've never seen her use any other cosmetics other than nail polish and perfume.

Nowadays there isn't just temporary make-up, but permanent make-up as well as cosmetic surgery for almost any part of the body. There is even digital photoshop/airbrushing of pictures and CGI in movies to change the appearance of a person. Would you consider haircuts, hairstyling, muscle toning, tattoos, or anything similar to "make-up"? Does it enhance your natural beauty? Men or women? Why do we feel the need to adjust our appearance? Is it our way of grasping towards perfection? Is it for ourselves or how we appear to others?

Mama shared this quote with my sister and me to teach us that we do not need to go to the extreme of enhancing our natural beauty because too much can take away from the "natural" part.

Research Connection:

"Over the past year, Google searches for 'Instagram filters that change your face' have increased by a staggering 100% alongside Dove recently finding that 85% of young girls have already edited their appearance by the time they're 13 years old."

"Back in 2020, Snapchat offered preliminary support for a proposed a new law in the UK which would force social platforms to add labels to any posted image that had been digitally altered or enhanced (the proposal is still under consideration), while Google has also removed default image re-touching in its Pixel devices after research showed that this can have negative psychological impacts."

Source: Hutchinson, A. (2022, June 27). *New report looks at the rise of Beauty Enhancement Trends and tools online*. Social

Media Today. https://www.socialmediatoday.com/news/new-report-looks-at-the-rise-of-beauty-enhancement-trends-and-tools-online/626176/

Key Takeaways:

To avoid self-esteem decline like some young people and adults today experience, my mother wanted my sister and me to know that our natural beauty is what matters. In other words, we are enough just as we are. And to be happy to look at the face looking back at us in the mirror. If we want to enhance it, we do not need to be drastic with make-up or any other forms of physical enhancements to be beautiful. With or without enhancements we are all beautiful in our own unique way.

Life Application:

*"When working with youth, when mentoring young people, or when supporting the young person in your life...**help them celebrate their natural beauty and the natural beauty of others around them.**"*

- If a young person shares that they want to or plan to make physical alterations to their appearance, express an interest in learning why.
- The objective is to assess their current state of self-worth and self-esteem. And how can you support them in building it up, if you find that their responses are revealing

some unhealthy beliefs about themselves?

- Having resources to support and educate young individuals can be beneficial. Discussing statistics with them regarding social media's impact on beauty standards might provide valuable insights. Tap into resources like beauty standards documentaries, etc.

- Informed young people are better able to navigate the complex world around them.

Mama Knows #18

"YOU DON'T GO BACKWARDS IN LIFE YOU ALWAYS GO FORWARD"

I THINK I WAS in high school when I first paid attention to Mama saying "You don't go backwards in life, you always go forward." This quote was deposited in me and I have been able to capitalize off it ever since. I remember hearing it in my head and saying it out loud in a prayer when I purchased my first property in December 2006...my one-bedroom/bath condo. I was so nervous yet excited. It was the first time I would be living on my own, paying all the bills, and being a 100% independent responsible adult. After closing, I prayed and asked God to help me maintain my new home that He had blessed me with. '"Mama said I don't go backwards in life, only forward. So, I need You, Lord, to help me always move forward so that I don't lose this place and have to go back to live with my parents!"

I did the same with other successful opportunities to move forward in life, such as relocating to Arizona and other blessings. My home purchase in Phoenix would be another example of a more recent blessing where I prayed the same prayer.

It's empowering to move forward like climbing a mountain to reach the top. Have you ever gone mountain hiking? When I first moved to Arizona that was one of the first things I did. It was not easy, but every step that I took kept me ascending higher up the mountain giving me a sense of "I can do it" to make it to the top. After persevering up the mountain and reaching the top, there was a beautiful view of the city that was well worth the struggle to get there. I also had a sense of accomplishment because there were indeed moments during the hike up that I wanted to turn around and go back(wards), but I endured the struggle to reach the top.

Research Connection:

"Imagine time running backwards. People would grow younger instead of older and, after a long life of gradual rejuvenation – unlearning everything they know – they would end as a twinkle in their parents' eyes. That's time as represented in a novel by science fiction writer Philip K Dick."

Source: Kitching, T., & Ucl. (2016, February 23). *What is time – and why does it move forward?*. Phys.org. https://phys.org/news/2016-02-what-is-time-and-why.html

Key Takeaways:

Time moves forward for the progression of life. We as people move forward for the advancement of our well-being. Going backwards doesn't have to be a negative, but I have found that *backwards* can either delay or prevent me from achieving goals. There would be an undoing of all that was attained if we all moved in reverse.

Life Application:

*"When working with youth, when mentoring young people, or when supporting the young person in your life...**instill forward movement**."*

- Life will get tough but we don't move closer to our goals without moving forward through adversity. Furthermore, once one goal is achieved, there are other things for us to accomplish in life. Artists, pianists, athletes, etc., they all become better at their craft by moving forward.

- Talk about this concept with your young people and ask them how they are "keeping it moving forward?"

Mama Knows #19

"Love doesn't change"

When I asked Mama about this quote she said, "No matter how much offense you experience, that doesn't change true love (God's love), but if we allow it, strength can be cultivated from our hurts or disappointments. It helps that I have the love of God inside of me because His love for us never changes despite ourselves which enables me to practice this same action with my neighbor." She always taught me that while you may dislike someone you love, your love for them never changes. It's that unconditional emotion and natural affection that is automatic. "Like" is fickle but love is constant. This is how Mama came to trust the Lord because He is constant, never changing His love. With people, she learned sometimes it's not the person's intent to cause the hurt so it is best practice to pray for them and bless them anyhow. We might not like how someone treats us, but God's word teaches us to ***"Love other people as much as you love yourself" (Matthew 22:39, EASY).***

Research Connection:

"Receiving unconditional love can also make a difference in emotional well-being. According to research from 2010, children who receive higher levels of affection from their parents or caregivers tend to have greater resilience in adulthood. They also tend to experience fewer mental health symptoms."

"Results from a 2013 study support the idea that loving children unconditionally improves their lifelong health and wellness. This suggests parental unconditional love could offer some protection against the harmful, often lingering effects of childhood trauma or abuse."

Source: Raypole, C. (2020, September 15). *Unconditional love: What it means and how to find it*. Healthline. https://www.healthline.com/health/relationships/unconditional-love#what-it-is

Key Takeaways:

Has unconditional love helped you overcome in any way? The research mentioned that receiving unconditional love benefits emotional health. My mother found strength in unconditional love to overcome hurts or traumas. *"Above all, have fervent, and unfailing love for one another, because love covers a multitude of sins [it overlooks unkindness and unselfishly seeks the best for others]."* ***(1 Peter 4:8, AMP)***

She developed a trust in God because of His love and because

He is love. *"We have come to know [by personal observation and experience], and have believed [with deep, consistent faith] the love which God has for us. God is love, and the one who abides in love abides in God, and God abides continually in him."* ***(1 John 4:16, AMP)***

Life Application:

"When working with youth, when mentoring young people, or when supporting the young person in your life... ***teach them the power of unconditional love.*** *"*

- Start by being an example and showing unconditional love to the young person in your life. Your demonstration is the best teaching tool.
- Then have a conversation with the young person about what unconditional love means. What it is and what it isn't. Use the scriptures shared as a foundation.

Mama Knows #20

"LAUGHING CATCHES"

MY DAD WAS A comic relief in our family during my childhood and he still is today. He would make jokes, do something silly, or point out something funny to make my sister and me laugh. From this, there were plenty of things I thought were funny as a child, but not everything I considered funny was meant to be funny or laughed at.

The most common thing I remember laughing about as a kid was anyone who looked 'funny' to me. Until one day Mama witnessed me laughing at someone. She asked, "What are you laughing at, Jaquay?" I told her and she said, "All right now, you shouldn't laugh at anyone who isn't intending to be funny...laughing catches."

I learned fast that a person who looked different or was injured, shamed, or less fortunate than I, was not someone to laugh at or about. That could easily be me or someone I cared for. "Catching" in the urban dictionary is defined as "mocking." What if I were the person being laughed at for something that wasn't meant to be funny? How would I feel being the brunt of someone's joke?

These are some things I had to think about in imagining myself on the other end of a good laugh. These questions helped me to be mindful of my neighbor to radiate kindness and not mockery. That's not to say there are not appropriate times of laughter with others or even regarding myself. These times of laughter would be in good humor and not destructive to myself or anyone else.

Research Connection:

"Upbringing, comfort level, and personality might explain why some can take pleasure in another's pain. Whatever the reason, scholars say the trademarks of humor can inspire laughter even in unfortunate situations."

"News and entertainment media's influence on the sensitivity of humor is in question...Youth, in particular, "have been numbed to the daily outpouring of violence, conflict, anger and atrocities in media," said Alan Ray, assistant professor of communication at the University of the Pacific."

"But M. Thomas Inge, humanities professor at Randolph-Macon College...said it's unfair to blame the media: "We came first. We built the media. It reflects us."

Source: Melendez, M. M. (2005, August 28). *Why do we find humor in others' pain?* The Seattle Times. https://www.seattle-times.com/news/why-do-we-find-humor-in-others-pain/

"Psychologists use the term "self-directed laughter" to describe laughing at oneself. In the early period of studying self-directed laughter, Allport (1961) identified the ability to laugh at oneself as having insight while still having a sense of self-acceptance. In other words, laughing at oneself is healthy when it is not motivated by self-demeaning drives. McGhee (1996, 2010) viewed laughing at oneself as healthy when you:

- Are able to look kindly at your weaknesses or mistakes
- See how embarrassing situations can be funny
- Can laugh without putting yourself down"

"It is important, however, to distinguish how laughter directed at oneself can cut both ways—increasing self-acceptance or self-disparagement. Sometimes self-directed humor is based on belittling or negative comments about oneself."

Source: Sreenivasan, S., & Weinberger, L. E. (2021). How laughing at yourself can be good for your well-being. https://www.psychologytoday.com/intl/blog/emotional-nourishment/202104/how-laughing-yourself-can-be-good-your-well-being

Key Takeaways:

Reflecting on the effects of laughter reveals that there can be positive or negative connotations regarding self or others. Healthily laughing at oneself can produce positive mental health outcomes. However, laughing at others in a teasing manner is unhealthy for everyone. One should never feel intimidated by laughter but instead be uplifted. Self-directed humor should be a way to strengthen self-esteem, not disparaging. Finding a healthy balance of when laughter is appropriate can be a beneficial component in healthy living.

Life Application:

*"When working with youth, when mentoring young people, or when supporting the young person in your life...**teach the difference in laughing at someone versus with someone.**"*

- Young people of all ages and backgrounds have either felt the sting of negative jokes or laughed at someone else being mocked. Use this topic to discuss how it feels to be laughed at negatively and how to show more compassion for others.

- Also, talk about ways in which laughing at oneself can be positive.

Mama Knows #21

"You live and you learn"

I remember times as a child, I'd share with Mama a mistake I made. She would lovingly say, "Well baby, you live and you learn." I understood this to mean that there are times in life when you have to go through a situation (live) or make a mistake to ***learn*** *how to navigate various experiences. It's similar to quote #16. I always think of this as 'experience is the best teacher' because you have to live out the situation to know how to learn from it. This quote can be applied to any life situation as we are constantly learning.*

My friend shared a story with me about her son. At age 11, he let his hair grow out and needed his hair lined. His grandfather who normally lines his hair was occupied the day he visited his grandparents, so he decided to line his own hair without telling anyone. He attempted to do his best with no help. When his mom saw him, she asked what happened. His hair was trimmed farther back from his natural hairline. One side of his hair also looked to be more shaved instead of lined. He told her that he had watched his grandfather line his hair plenty of times and it looked easy. Since he knew where his grandfather kept the clippers, he thought he'd do it himself (Quote #2...nothing beats a failure but a try). Unfortunately, his attempt to do his own lining with no experience did not turn out so well. You live and you learn.

Research Connection:

"Experience is not the best teacher; **evaluated** experience is", Howard G. Hendricks explained.

Source: Oppong, T. (2021, September 9). *Learning truly begins when you practice in the real world.* Medium. https://medium.com/personal-growth/learning-truly-begins-when-you-practice-in-the-real-world-3b1831a421e9

Key Takeaways:

When we take time to **evaluate** and reflect on our experiences we can learn from them. Pay attention to the *do's* and the *don'ts* asking ourselves "How did an experience result in a successful outcome or an ineffective one." *You live and you learn* develops maturity and wisdom as we go through the journey of life.

Life Application:

*"When working with youth, when mentoring young people, or when supporting the young person in your life...**teach young people how to evaluate their experiences.**"*

- Teach the young person in your life how to be more reflective. Journaling can be a useful tool to teach introspection.

- From that point, instruct them on assessing their experiences by contemplating the positive and negative outcomes derived from life's events.

Mama Knows #22

"Better late than never"

I have a passion for children that has existed since I was a little girl. I remember thinking how I loved children so much that I wanted to help them. "I'm going to be a pediatrician when I grow up," I proclaimed. During my junior year of high school, I was preparing to apply to colleges that would begin my journey of becoming a pediatrician. Mama asked me if I was sure that was what I wanted to do. We talked about it and she suggested that I get a technical trade first then if I still had a desire to be a Pediatrician, I could move forward with that process. I thought that was a good idea so I got my two-year technical trade and started working in the IT industry in 2000.

Over time, I no longer wanted to be a pediatrician. But I still had a deep love for children. I asked myself...did I make the right decision? Years passed and my interactions with children were with family and my friends' kids. I enjoyed spending time with them whenever I could. Then in 2014 I relocated to Arizona, joined my new church home in 2015, and started volunteering in the children's ministry. This was such a great experience and my passion blossomed. I was asked to lead the ministry for the Nursery and Pre-K in 2016. I prayed about it and God confirmed. This decision was one of the most fulfilling and flourishing experiences in my life.

In 2020, I was encouraged by a vision from the Holy Spirit to start a part-time childcare business and He showed me that my clients would be the families that I was serving in the church ministry. From the start, the business was a success, so much so that I had to pause it in 2022 with permission from the Spirit of Counsel. I was still working full-time and there were other projects I was to embark on. It felt odd to me to temporarily stop a flourishing childcare business, but by seeking God in prayer, I understood that there was a time and season for everything. Through ministry to business, I have come to realize that caring for the youth was just a later plan in my life rather than a never plan.

Research Connection:

"People make plans for what they will do, but it is the Lord who leads them in the right way." **(Proverbs 16:9, EASY)**

"There is a right time for everything. Everything that we do on the earth has a proper time." **(Ecclesiastes 3:1, EASY)**

"You can make many plans, but the Lord's purpose will prevail." **(Proverbs 19:21, NLT)**

Key Takeaways:

Have you ever had it in your mind that it was too late to fulfill a dream or goal you'd been carrying for a while (never put off tomorrow what you can do today, Quote # 14)? Remember that positive idea or thought you've had in your heart? Or those plans such as going back to school, traveling, writing a book, changing careers, cleaning the house, quitting smoking, etc.... It's not too late to go for it.

During the 2023 Thanksgiving holiday, my mother mentioned that she was preparing a variety of Thanksgiving dishes for family and friends. They were not gathering together but just wanted her cooking to be part of their Thanksgiving dinner. I suggested that maybe she should start a catering business since everyone loves her cooking so much. She replied, "Yeah right, not at my age."

And right before I could respond with, *remember what you always said*...she finished her statement with, "I know, it's better late than never."

I laughed and said, "You took the words right out of my mouth!" I suggested some encouraging ideas on how she could begin catering on a small scale as a hobby and then observe how it develops from there.

Life Application:

*"When working with youth, when mentoring young people, or when supporting the young person in your life...**teach them that some dreams may happen quickly but others may come later in life.**"*

- How can you foster perseverance, patience, and the concept of God's timing in a young person?

Mama Knows #23

"You get what you pay for"

I love wearing medium-sized hoop earrings, but I'm often misplacing them or losing one hoop. So, I buy the inexpensive cheaper gold-plated ones that cost about $10-$20 depending on the size and style. I get so bothered when I have the earrings for a short time and see some of the gold coming off in spots leaving the metal exposed. Then I think...you get what you pay for.

There are just some things worth paying a sensible price depending on craftsmanship, design, and value. When I still lived in Chicago, I would visit my parents on Sunday afternoons after our church service. One Sunday, Dad had gone to the store after the service. When he came home, he was excited to tell my sister and me that he got a pack of hotdogs for ninety-nine cents! My sister and I looked at each other, confused.

I asked Dad why he would buy such low quality hotdogs. Mama previously worked at Vienna Beef Co so she ordered cases of hotdogs and that was the brand we would eat or the Best Kosher brand. Both were considered to be good quality hotdogs and cost more than ninety-nine cents, for sure.

Dad boiled him a couple of those ninety-nine-cent hotdogs, prepped them on the bun with some mustard then came to sit down in the den with my sister and me to watch TV. We both watched him in eager anticipation of his reaction. With a smile on his face, he took a bite out of one of the hotdogs. As he started chewing, the smile began to droop. Then came that official frown confirming exactly what my sister and I suspected. I started laughing loudly and so did my sister.

An expression of disgust was written all over Dad's face, but he kept trying to eat the rest of the hotdog. "Daddy, why don't you stop eating that and just throw it in the garbage, you know it's not good," I insisted. My dad is infamous for not throwing anything out, especially food, which he considers "wasting."

Well shortly after my remarks, he got up and threw the ninety-nine-cent hotdogs in the garbage. I yelled, "Don't forget about the uncooked ones!" As he came back in the den to sit down with his face frowned up, I said, "You know Mama always says, you get what you pay for." It was one of the funniest moments with my dad that I will never forget.

Research Connection:

"Multiple studies have shown a correlation between product pricing and customer satisfaction. A study conducted by the Journal of Consumer Research found that consumers who paid higher prices for a product perceived it to be of higher quality and reported higher levels of satisfaction compared to those who paid lower prices for the same product."

"According to a study published in the Journal of Consumer Research, consumers tend to believe that higher-priced products are made with better materials, have superior craftsmanship, or offer added features...This perception can influence their purchasing decisions and overall satisfaction with the product."

Source: Lee, S. (2023, September 18). *The meaning and origins of the "you get what you pay for" meme*. Own Your Own Future. https://www.ownyourownfuture.com/you-get-what-you-pay-for-meme/

Key Takeaways:

Those of us who shop for apparel, jewelry, food, vehicles, houses, etc. can likely determine the best bang for our buck and identify the worth of the item being purchased. Though our perception of price plays a part in what we decide to purchase, our discernment is also a determining aspect for us to conclude that we get what we pay for.

Life Application:

*"When working with youth, when mentoring young people, or when supporting the young person in your life...**teach young people about making wise purchasing decisions.**"*

- Teach young people when it is important to spend more on high-quality items and when it's wise to cut costs and choose a lower-cost product.
- Also, think about ways this skill set can transfer to other

life choices (quality over quantity).

Mama Knows #24

"Don't buy the first or last item at a grocery store"

Don't buy the first or last product generally applies mostly to edible products for me but can be applied to other items as well. Grocery shopping has always been a fun experience for me growing up and still is today. Mama made it fun from talking to the workers, critiquing the food and produce, to checking out with the cashier. If she would have me grab something we needed, she would be sure to say, "Don't take the first one, get the one behind it, or reach back and get one from far back." If it was the only item left, she would tell me not to get that one.

Don't buy the first or last item...sounds like a myth, right? Well, it's not. There is wisdom there. Typically, the first row or first couple of rows of items on a shelf are the ones that have been on the shelf the longest...they likely were previously towards the back rows, but people don't tend to reach to the back. We generally grab what's right in front, so those items in the back get pulled to the front when the fresher or newer items are placed in the back rows. Buying the last item, that's a little different. Is this item expired? Was it returned? Is it damaged? I remember buying some flour once. It was the last item on the shelf for the brand I bought. I was a little hesitant, checking the expiration to be sure it was still good. In the back of my mind, I was thinking I know Mama said...don't buy the last one. Well, I did and when I opened it, there were those little flour bugs in it. I immediately said out loud... "Mama knows best." Could it have been a coincidence...I don't believe in coincidences. What I know is I make a point to not purchase the first or the last item at the grocery store.

Research Connection:

"A team of psychologists at the University of California, Riverside / Researchers, led by David A. Rosenbaum, a distinguished professor of psychology, devised an experimental task that measured reaction times when participants chose between two possibilities: Act just for action's sake or clear the mind by deciding early what to do."

"Students at UCR who participated in the experiments were asked to make yes-no decisions on the task, which involved a set of numbers they were shown. They were then asked to make yes-no decisions again in case they had changed their minds."

"The researchers found the first-response reaction times were longer than the second-response reaction times. In other words, people tend to think before they act rather than act before they think."

“In our experiments, participants took longer for the first choice than the second and rarely changed their minds, even when we emphasized second response accuracy,” Rosenbaum said.

"This led us to conclude that our participants wanted to make up their minds as soon as possible rather than act quickly and then have to think or rethink. This suggests that even though people engage in seemingly impulsive decision-making, they may actually be predisposed to curtail it."

Source: Pittalwala, I. (2022, October 5). *Do you act before you think or Think before you act?*. Neuroscience News. https://neurosciencenews.com/precrastination-predisposition-21578/

Key Takeaways:

Remember those notes in elementary school that you passed to the boy or girl you liked or maybe you received one...Do you like me...yes or no? As a kid, did you stop to think about it or did you immediately circle your response? Taking time to think about a choice, an answer, or a decision is most often better in the long run than just quickly responding. We might not have the opportunity to change our minds once we respond depending on the situation. Assessing the pros and cons could prevent regret later. Decision-making doesn't always have to be well thought out for those simple routine selections we tend to make on a more regular basis, especially when we already have a "rule of thumb" to work with like Mama's grocery store hack. Being mindful of the weight of the desire, question, or offer can determine how fast or how slow our response time should be.

Life Application:

"When working with youth, when mentoring young people, or when

*supporting the young person in your life...**equip them with decision-making skill sets.**"*

- Oftentimes, there is a systematic process to most things in life. Although some rules can be broken to forge new paths, a young person won't know when to pivot if they don't understand the rules or process from the start. Teach young people how to navigate diverse spaces and why certain systems are in place.

Mama Knows #25

"Don't idolize anything other than God or that thing will be taken away"

As a teenager, I was really into my hair. Keeping my hair looking good. Whether I did it in a style myself or went to a salon to get it done, I made sure I tended to it because I loved my hair. Mom would often find me looking in the mirror doing something with my hair.

One day she told me to be careful with my hair. I didn't know what she meant so I asked her. She told me to be careful not to idolize my hair or anything else other than God because it can be taken away. I didn't understand and said, "I'm not idolizing my hair, I'm just doing it and making sure it looks good." I remember her saying you spend a lot of time focusing on your hair. I can't remember how long after that conversation I experienced a scary moment later that made the light bulb come on.

I had my first car accident at age 16. It was at night and I had just gotten off work from the movie theater. It had rained that night and I had driven my dad's car that we used for short trips. On my way home I made a left turn off a side street to the main road when the car started sliding out of control. Instead of hitting the brakes, I accidentally accelerated and crashed into a light pole. I was so scared but was able to call my parents from a pay phone to tell them what happened.

When I got home, our neighbor asked me if I hit my head because he saw the windshield was cracked on the driver's side. I told him I didn't think so. Well, when I got into the house and went to look at myself in the bathroom mirror, there was glass in the top center of my head! I began picking the glass out and my hair started coming out too. As I looked at the cut strands of hair in my hand, tears began to fall. I was crying that ugly "I can't believe this," kind of cry. As soon as I saw the hair in my hand, what came to the forefront of my mind? "Don't idolize anything other than God or that thing will be taken away from you."

Mama heard my cry and came running hysterically asking what was wrong. Crying intensely, I was able to utter...my hair, my hair. She immediately embraced me and held me gently saying, "It's ok Jaquay. Mama knows. It will grow back, but remember what Mama said about God. He wants to be number one in your life."

In this moment I understood what it meant to "idolize" something. This set the stage for me going forward as I walk through life to only idolize/worship God. What an amazing journey it has been. Over the years, there have been other idols I was unaware of in my heart like self-reliance, credit cards, and my job to name a few. Gradually, God has been ever so gentle in bringing them to my attention. Through prayer, He removes them and helps me recognize to put Him first.

While we're on the subject...can you identify any areas in your own life that you obsess over but may not think of as idols?

Research Connection:

"God spoke, and these were his words: 'I am the LORD your God who brought you out of Egypt, where you were slaves. Worship no god but me. Do not make for yourselves images of anything in heaven or on earth or in the water under the earth. Do not bow down to any idol or worship it, because I am the LORD your God and I tolerate no rivals. I bring punishment on those who hate me and on their descendants down to the third and fourth generation. But, I show my love to thousands of generations of those who love me and obey my laws." ***(Exodus 20:1-10, GNT)***

"Teacher, which commandment in the law is the greatest?" Jesus answered him, 'Love the Lord your God with every passion of your heart, with all the energy of your being, and with every thought that is within you.' This is the great and supreme commandment." ***(Matthew 22:36-38, TPT)***

"Little children (believers, dear ones), guard yourselves from idols – [false teachings, moral compromises, and anything that would take God's place in your heart]." ***(1 John 5:21, AMP)***

"Therefore, my beloved, run [keep far, far away] from [any sort of] idolatry [and that includes loving anything more than God, or participating in anything that leads to sin and enslaves the soul]." ***(1 Corinthians 10:14, AMP)***

Key Takeaways:

Worship no other god but the true God. Did I "worship" my hair? I didn't think I did at the time, but maybe there would come a point where vanity would permeate in me and likely spiral out of control. When I thought about it, I recognized that I didn't care as much that I had just undergone an actual **car accident, could have gotten really hurt,** or that I totaled my dad's car, but that my "hair" was coming out. I don't consider what happened to me a punishment from God but a consequence of the accident that occurred which got my attention to understand idolatry. I learned to love God more than anything or anyone else in the world.

Life Application:

*"When working with youth, when mentoring young people, or when supporting the young person in your life...**inspire them to love God more than anything or anyone else**."*

- Share the mentioned Bible verses with the young person or any other related verses.
- Ask if they have any questions.
- Attempt to answer any questions or refer to someone/resources who can offer more insight.
- Ask them what are the things and/or the people they love.
- Follow by asking them how they can cultivate their love for God above anything else in their lives.

Conclusion

Mama Knows Best is more than just a collection of quotes; it's a testament to the enduring power of maternal wisdom and the profound impact it can have on shaping the lives of the next generation. As we come to the end of this journey together, let's carry forward the lessons learned and the insights gained, not just for ourselves, but as beacons of guidance for those who follow in our footsteps.

May the wisdom of Mama's quotes continue to inspire, uplift, and empower you all to nurture meaningful relationships with the young souls entrusted to your care. I pray you embrace the legacy of love, wisdom, and compassion that my mother has bestowed upon us, knowing that with God's guidance, we can navigate life's challenges and empower the youth to reach their fullest potential.

About the author

Jaquay Reed is a passionate advocate for youth empowerment and mentorship.

In 2022, Jaquay founded Created For Greatness, a dynamic outreach program tailored for young girls aged 9 to 16. Through this initiative, she dedicates herself to mentoring and guiding young girls to recognize their inherent purpose and potential, equipping them with the tools to embark on a journey toward greatness from an early age. Her commitment to nurturing the next generation is rooted in her belief that every young person deserves the opportunity to discover and pursue their unique path to success.

Jaquay's dedication to youth development extends beyond her outreach program. With over 8 years of experience serving as a servant leader for the Nursery and Pre-K ministry at her church, she has played an integral role in providing a nurturing and supportive environment for children to grow spiritually and emotionally. Her faithful service on Sundays reflects her unwavering commitment to instilling values of love, compassion, and humility in the hearts of young minds.

In addition to her hands-on involvement in youth mentorship,

Jaquay has also contributed her insights to a collaborative book project, where she shared her expertise on the topic of Building In Humility. Through her various endeavors, Jaquay continues to inspire and empower young people to embrace their potential and pursue their dreams with confidence and purpose.

Residing in Arizona, she finds joy in exploring nature through hiking trails and indulging her love for cinema. However, her greatest passion lies in culinary adventures, as she delights in exploring restaurants and savoring delectable cuisine.

Acknowledgements

This is a dream come true and I want to start by thanking the Most High God, my everything, my Foundation. Thank You Jesus the Head of my life for giving me the courage, words, opportunity, and confidence to write this book. Thank You Holy Spirit for direction, conviction, and approval in writing this book.

I want to especially thank my mother, Rosie O'Neal Reed, who I'm dedicating this book to. You are an inspiration to me. I could not have done this without you, your love, or your encouragement. I want you to know that I am extremely grateful to God that you are my mama. Without you, I would not be the woman that I am today. Your smile, your joy, and your desire to love is so contagious. You have instilled those things in me. I admire your strength, your giving, and so much more. Your wisdom and teachings from childhood have helped mold and shape me, plus they are embedded in me. You have been and continue to be an inspiration to me as my wonderful, loving, beautiful, kind mama. I praise the Lord for you and appreciate you for being you, for caring for me, loving me, protecting me, and always being there for me.

To my dad, William C. Reed, your role in my life has made a crucial impact on who I am today. Thank you for always supporting me and believing in me. You continuously bless me with your love, encouragement, and protection. I appreciate how you have always kept an open mind and provided constructive criticism when I needed it.

To my sister, Elaine Reed, thank you for the role you played in helping me get here. Your words of wisdom and your love are greatly appreciated. If not for your humor and mild temperament to balance me out, I would be coo-coo for cocoa puffs!

A very special thanks to my editor and writing coach, Sinyon Ducksworth, who has given me that extra boost of confidence as an author. This journey with you has been educational, humbling, and exciting. Thank you for your grace and patience along the way. I look forward to working with you on my future projects.

OTHER BOOKS
by Jaquay

How to Grow in Humility

review in my blog

www.jalaree.com

www.ingramcontent.com/pod-product-compliance
Lightning Source LLC
LaVergne TN
LVHW090616110826
845146LV00001B/409